Explore the Solar System

The Sun
and Other
Stars

WORLD
BOOK
a Scott Fetzer company
Chicago
www.worldbookonline.com

World Book, Inc.
233 N. Michigan Avenue
Chicago, IL 60601
U.S.A.

For information about other World Book publications, visit our Web site at **http://www.worldbookonline.com** or call **1-800-WORLDBK (967-5325).**

For information about sales to schools and libraries, call **1-800-975-3250 (United States),** or **1-800-837-5365 (Canada).**

Library of Congress Cataloging-in-Publication Data
The sun and other stars.
   p. cm. -- (Explore the solar system)
   Summary: "An introduction to the sun and other stars for primary and intermediate grade students with information about their features and exploration. Includes charts and diagrams, a list of highlights for each chapter, fun facts, glossary, resource list, and index"--Provided by publisher.
   Includes index.
   ISBN 978-0-7166-9539-4
   1. Sun--Juvenile literature. 2. Stars--Juvenile literature. 3. Solar system--Juvenile literature. I. World Book, Inc.
   QB521.5.S864 2011
   523.7--dc22
                              2009038005

ISBN 978-0-7166-9533-2 (set)

Printed in China by Leo Paper Products Ltd.,
   Heshan, Guangdong
1st printing August 2010

Staff

Executive Committee

Vice President and Chief Financial Officer: Donald D. Keller

Vice President and Editor in Chief: Paul A. Kobasa

Vice President, Licensing & Business Development: Richard Flower

Chief Technology Officer: Tim Hardy

Managing Director, International: Benjamin Hinton

Director, Human Resources: Bev Ecker

Editorial:

Associate Director, Supplementary Publications: Scott Thomas

Managing Editor, Supplementary Publications: Barbara A. Mayes

Senior Editor, Supplementary Publications: Kristina A. Vaicikonis

Manager, Research, Supplementary Publications: Cheryl Graham

Manager, Contracts & Compliance (Rights & Permissions): Loranne K. Shields

Editor: Michael DuRoss

Writer: Lori Meek Schuldt

Indexer: David Pofelski

Graphics and Design:

Manager: Tom Evans

Coordinator, Design Development and Production: Brenda B. Tropinski

Associate Designer: Matt Carrington

Contributing Photographs Editor: Carol Parden

Pre-Press and Manufacturing:

Director: Carma Fazio

Manufacturing Manager: Steven K. Hueppchen

Production/Technology Manager: Anne Fritzinger

Proofreader: Emilie Schrage

Picture Acknowledgments:
Cover front: NASA/ESA; NASA/JPL-Caltech/Harvard-Smithsonian CfA; Cover back: NASA/JPL-Caltech/UCLA.

© Don Dixon 24; HEIC 38; © Robert Hurt/IPAC 57; National Optical Astronomy Observatory 21; NASA 1, 17, 19, 23, 30, 34; NASA/CXC/MIT 53; NASA/CXC/SAO/STScl 49, 50; NASA/ESA/Hubble Heritage Team 33, 37, 38, 44; NASA/JPL 41; NASA/SOHO/ESA 9, 10, 43; NASA/STScl/AURA 5, 28; NASA/Transition Region & Coronal Explorer 13; © Lynette Cook, Photo Researchers 46; SPL, Photo Researchers 20; © Frank Zullo, Photo Researchers 17; Royal Swedish Academy of Sciences 19; Digital Sky Survey/STScl 26;

Illustrations: WORLD BOOK illustration by Matt Carrington 15, 54; WORLD BOOK illustration by Steve Karp 6; WORLD BOOK illustration by Rob Wood

Astronomers use different kinds of photos to learn about such objects in space as planets. Many photos show an object's natural color. Other photos use false colors. Some false-color images show types of light the human eye cannot normally see. Others have colors that were changed to highlight important features. When appropriate, the captions in this book state whether a photo uses natural or false color.

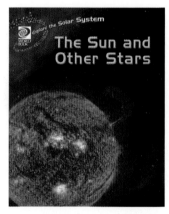

Cover image:
An immense burst of energy flares from the outermost surface of the sun, the central star in the solar system.

Contents

If a word is printed in **bold letters that look like this,** that word's meaning is given in the glossary on pages 60-61.

What Is a Star?

A **star** is a shining object in space. The sun is the star in the center of the **solar system.** In the night sky, the stars look like twinkling points of light. The sun looks like a huge ball of light because it is so near to Earth.

Stars come in many sizes and types. Most stars produce a tremendous amount of energy, chiefly in the form of light and heat. Most stars are made of gas and an electrically charged, gas-like material called **plasma.**

There may be as many as 10 billion trillion stars in the **universe.** But on a dark night far away from city lights, we can see only about 3,000 of them without using binoculars or a telescope.

Stars are not spread out evenly in space. Some are found in large groups called star clusters. These groups are held together by **gravity,** the effect of the force of attraction between them.

Stars and star clusters are grouped into huge structures called **galaxies.** The sun is in the

Highlights

- Stars are shining objects in space that produce light and heat.
- Most stars are made of gas and a substance called plasma.
- There may be about 10 billion trillion stars.
- Stars are often found in such formations as star clusters, galaxies, and binary systems.

Milky Way Galaxy. The Milky Way has more than 100 billion stars. Galaxies also tend to be grouped together in clusters.

A star cluster in a natural-color photograph

More than half of all stars are part of a binary system. A binary system is a pair of closely spaced stars that **orbit** each other. The sun does not belong to a binary system.

Where Is the Sun?

← **Sun**

Mercury   Venus   Earth   Mars

Jupiter

The sun is the **star** closest to Earth. The sun is, on average, about 93 million miles (150 million kilometers) from Earth. Sunlight takes only about 8 minutes to reach Earth. That is because light travels at a speed of 186,282 miles (299,792 kilometers) per second.

The sun is the only star in the **solar system.** Earth and the other **planets** of the solar system **orbit** the sun. Other objects, including **asteroids** and **comets,** also travel around the sun.

The sun's location in the solar system
(Planets are shown to scale.)

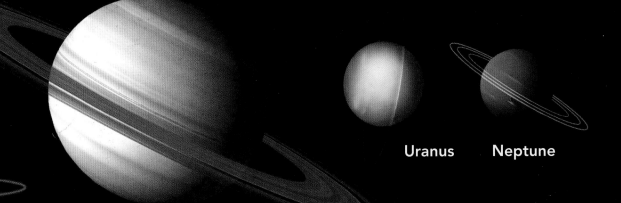

Saturn

Uranus   Neptune

The sun is about 25,000 **light-years** from the center of the Milky Way Galaxy. (A light-year is the distance light travels in one year. It equals about 5.88 trillion miles [9.46 trillion kilometers].) It takes the sun about 250 million years to revolve once around the center of the Milky Way.

Highlights

- The sun is the center of the solar system and the star closest to Earth.
- The sun is about 93 million miles (150 million kilometers) from Earth and about 25,000 light-years from the center of the Milky Way Galaxy.
- It takes about 8 minutes for sunlight to reach Earth.

How Big Is the Sun?

The sun is the largest object in the **solar system.** It contains 99.8 percent of all the **mass** (amount of **matter**) in the solar system. In other words, the sun has more mass than all of the **planets,** moons, **asteroids,** and other objects in the solar system put together. The sun has about 333,000 times as much mass as Earth does.

The sun's **radius** (the distance from its center to its surface) is about 432,000 miles (695,500 kilometers). That distance is more than 100 times as long as Earth's radius. About 1 million Earths could fit inside the sun.

To picture how these sizes compare, imagine Earth as an adult person and the sun as a building. If Earth's radius were the height of a person, then the sun's radius would be about the height of a 60-story skyscraper.

To us, the sun seems huge—and it is. But for a **star,** the sun is average-sized and fairly usual.

Highlights

- The sun is the largest object in the solar system.
- It contains 99.8 percent of the total mass of the solar system.
- The sun's radius is about 870,000 miles (1.4 million kilometers)—more than 100 times as large as Earth's.
- Compared with other stars, the sun is of average size.

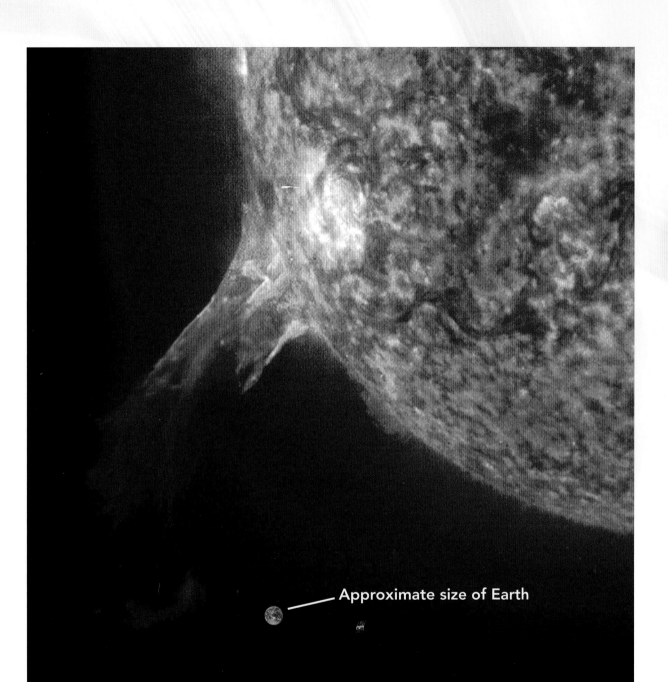

Approximate size of Earth

A tiny photograph of Earth is combined with a false-color photograph of the sun to show their relative sizes. The sun is so much larger than Earth that in a photograph made to scale, Earth would be too small to see.

How Hot Is the Sun?

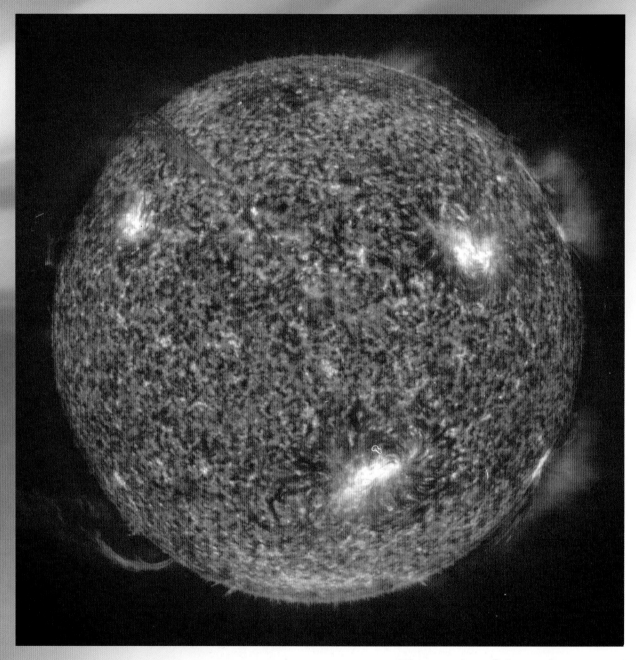

The sun in a false-color
photograph

The sun is extremely hot. The outer part that we can see has a temperature of about 10,600 °F (5500 °C). That is about 50 times hotter than the boiling temperature of water.

Astronomers express the sun's temperature in another way. They measure the very high temperature of the sun and other **stars** using a metric unit called the **Kelvin** (abbreviated K). The Kelvin scale starts at absolute zero. Scientists think that at this temperature, **atoms** have the least possible energy. On the Fahrenheit and Celsius scales, absolute zero is equal to -459.67 °F, or -273.15 °C.

The surface of the sun has a temperature of about 5800 K. However, temperatures in the sun's **core** reach more than 15 million K, or 27 million °F (15 million °C).

The sun looks yellow because of the temperature at its surface. Cooler stars are reddish. Hotter stars look bluish.

Highlights

- The sun's outermost layer has a temperature of about 10,000 °F (5500 °C), or 5800 K.
- K is an abbreviation for Kelvin, the metric unit astronomers use to express the high temperature of the sun and other stars.
- The temperature in the sun's core is more than 15 million K.

Where Does the Sun's Energy Come From?

The sun produces energy through a process called **nuclear fusion.** The sun, like most **stars,** is made up mainly of **atoms** of the chemical element **hydrogen,** the lightest element. Chemical elements contain only one kind of atom, the basic unit of **matter.** In nuclear fusion, the *nuclei* (centers) of lighter atoms *fuse* (combine) to form the nuclei of heavier atoms.

Fun Fact

It takes about 1 million years for the energy released by nuclear fusion reactions in the sun's core to work its way to the surface and be released as heat and light.

Highlights

- The sun makes energy through nuclear fusion.
- In nuclear fusion, the nuclei of lighter atoms combine to form the nuclei of heavier atoms.
- The process of nuclear fusion releases energy.

Nuclei have a positive electric charge, so they tend to *repel* (push away) one another. But in the sun's core, the temperature is very high and conditions are *dense* (crowded). There, the nuclei of hydrogen are fused to create the nuclei of helium, a slightly heavier chemical element.

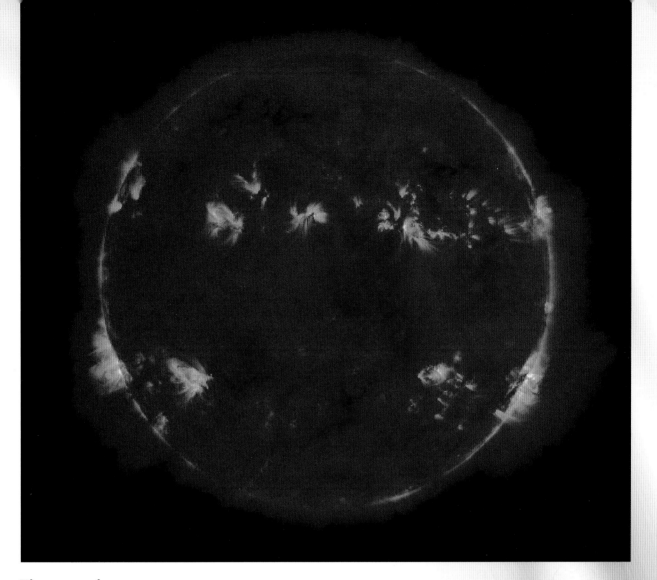

The sun releases energy in loops and streams of gas in a photograph taken in ultraviolet light.

When nuclei fuse, a small amount of their **mass** (amount of matter) turns to energy. Most of the energy is released as visible light and infrared rays. Visible light is the light we can see. Infrared rays are heat rays that warm our **planet.** Within the sun and most other stars, nuclear fusion takes place constantly. As a result, stars produce a steady stream of light and heat.

What Is the Sun Made Of?

About 94 percent of the sun **mass** consists of **atoms** of the chemical element **hydrogen.** The element helium, which is slightly heavier than hydrogen, makes up nearly 6 percent of the sun. Other elements in the sun include oxygen, carbon, neon, nitrogen, iron, and silicon.

The sun is so hot that none of its **matter** exists in solid or liquid form. All of the sun's matter exists as a gas or as a gas-like form called **plasma.** When a gas is heated to a very hot temperature, the atoms that make up the gas come apart. This leaves plasma. Plasma consists of **ions**—atoms with an electric charge—and **electrons,** electrically charged atomic particles. The inside of the sun and most of its atmosphere consist of plasma.

The sun consists of several zones, or layers. At the center of

Highlights

- The sun is made mostly of hydrogen.
- The sun also contains helium and small amounts of other elements.
- The hydrogen, helium, and other elements in the sun exist as either gas or a gas-like form of matter called plasma.

Inside the Sun

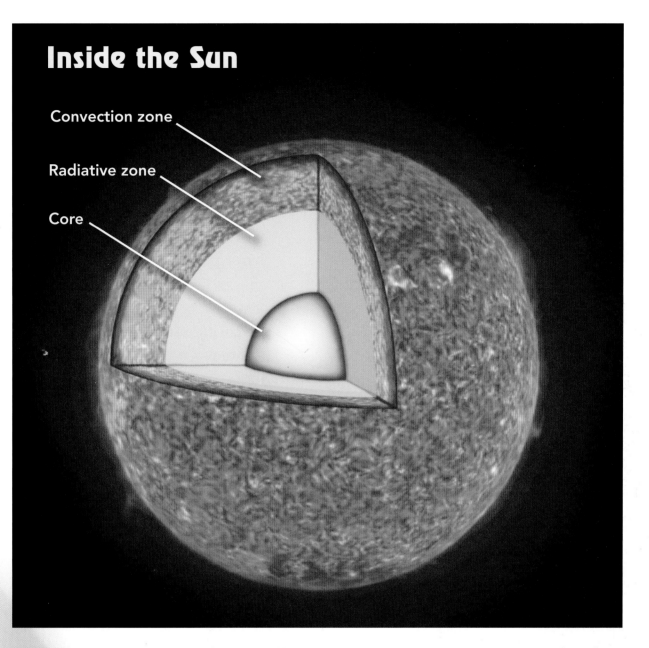

Convection zone

Radiative zone

Core

the sun is the **core.** Almost all the **nuclear fusion** in the sun takes place in the core. Energy flows outward from the core through the radiative zone. The convection zone consists of violently churning gases. It extends to the surface. The sun's **atmosphere** begins above the convection zone.

What Is the Sun's Atmosphere Like?

The sun's **atmosphere** has several layers. The photosphere is the lowest part of the atmosphere. It rises from the **star's** surface. The photosphere sends out the sunlight that we see on Earth.

Above the photosphere is the chromosphere. Temperatures rise dramatically in this layer of the sun's atmosphere.

The layer above the chromosphere is called the transition region. In this zone, temperatures vary greatly from one place to another. Some areas absorb energy from the chromosphere. They remain cooler than areas that receive energy from the corona, the outermost layer of the sun.

Highlights

- The sun's atmosphere is made up of four layers—the photosphere, the chromosphere, the transition region, and the corona.
- The sunlight that we see comes from the photosphere.
- The hottest layer, the corona, extends out into space in fiery loops.

The corona is the hottest layer of the sun's atmosphere. The corona is so hot that its gas atoms lose their **electrons** and become electrically charged **ions**. These particles continually flow out into space as the solar wind.

The moon passes in front of the sun during an eclipse, revealing the glow of the corona in a false-color photograph.

The sun appears in ultraviolet light, a form of light invisible to human eyes, in a photograph by the Solar and Heliospheric Observatory (right). Such photographs allows scientists to measure the temperature of the corona.

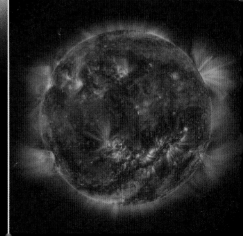

What Activities Occur In the Sun's Atmosphere?

The sun is a magnet. The region of magnetism around the sun is called its **magnetic field.** The sun's magnetic field becomes especially strong in small areas on the surface and in the **atmosphere.** The **matter** in these regions forms such features as **sunspots, solar flares,** and **coronal mass ejections.**

Sunspots are dark, circular features on the surface. The number of sunspots and the areas where sunspots appear vary over a period that lasts for about 11 years. This period is known as the sunspot cycle.

A solar flare is a sudden brightening of a part of the solar atmosphere. Flares release a tremendous amount of magnetic energy. A solar flare causes a huge increase in the temperature of the corona—to about 10 million Kelvin or even higher.

Highlights

- The sun's magnetic field causes several kinds of eruptions.
- Sunspots are dark circular areas on the surface of the sun.
- Solar flares are a sudden brightening of a part of the surface.
- Coronal mass ejections are eruptions of a large volume of the corona into space.

Large loops of gas that erupt from the sun's outer atmosphere can reach as high as 311,000 miles (500,000 kilometers).

Large eruptions of material from the corona into space are called coronal mass ejections. These eruptions occur when a part of the magnetic field erupts from the sun. This eruption sweeps a large volume of the corona into space, creating a cloud of gas.

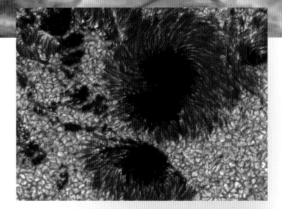

Dark features on the surface of the sun, called sunspots, appear in a false-color photograph.

How Do Scientists Study the Sun?

For hundreds of years, scientists have used a variety of tools and methods to study the sun. Telescopes were the earliest tools. The first telescopes were made in the early 1600's. Within a few years, such scientists as the Italian **astronomer** Galileo (*GAL uh LAY oh* or *GAL uh LEE oh*) were using telescopes to study the sun and **planets** of the **solar system.**

Telescopes gradually became bigger and better. Special devices were developed to keep astronomers from damaging their eyes when observing the sun. These devices included filters for telescopes and eye protection for observers.

Solar observers began taking photographs of the sun in 1858. In the late 1800's, astronomers began using an instrument called a spectroheliograph to photograph the sun in different colors of the **spectrum.** The spectrum is a band of visible light or other kind of **radiation** arranged according to the length of its waves. (A rainbow is a spectrum.) Such photos revealed that the sun's inner **atmosphere** was layered.

In the 1960's, scientists found that the sun vibrates like a bell that is continually being struck. This discovery allowed scientists to use these vibrations to study the sun's interior.

Astronomer George Ellery Hale (left) invented the spectrohelio-graph, an instrument for photographing the sun in different colors of the spectrum.

A mirror at the McMath-Pierce Telescope Facility near Tucson, Arizona, (above) helps astronomers track the sun.

Highlights

- The first instruments scientists used to study the sun were simple telescopes.
- Later, scientists developed special devices to protect their eyes when viewing the sun.
- Photographs taken in the 1800's revealed that the sun's atmosphere consists of layers.
- In the 1960's, scientists learned about the interior of the sun by studying its vibrations.

How Are Satellites Used to Study the Sun?

Since the 1960's, scientists have used **satellites** and spacecraft to study the sun. In 1980, the United States National Aeronautics and Space Administration (NASA) launched the Solar Maximum Mission Satellite. In 1994, the space probe Ulysses became the first craft to observe the sun from an **orbit** that passed

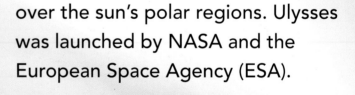

Fun Fact

Although SOHO was launched in 1995 to study the sun, by 2003, the spacecraft had discovered at least 620 comets, more than any other source.

Highlights

- Since the 1960's, scientists have used satellites and spacecraft as well as telescopes to study the sun.
- Since 1995, an orbiting telescope called SOHO has been taking pictures of the sun every 10 to 15 minutes.
- In 2004, NASA's Genesis spacecraft brought back samples of the solar wind.

over the sun's polar regions. Ulysses was launched by NASA and the European Space Agency (ESA).

NASA and the ESA also maintain the Solar and Heliospheric Observatory (SOHO). Launched in 1995, this orbiting telescope takes images of the sun every 10 to 15 minutes. Another spacecraft launched by NASA, Genesis, returned to Earth in 2004 with samples of the solar wind.

In 2006, NASA and the Japanese Space Agency each launched missions to study the effects of the sun's **magnetic field** on Earth. NASA's STEREO (Solar Terrestrial Relations Observatory) uses two satellites to study **coronal mass ejections (CME's)**. These eruptions disturb Earth's **magnetic field**. CME's sometimes produce magnetic storms that can damage satellites and spacecraft and interfere with electrical equipment on Earth. Japan's Hinode probe studies how the sun's magnetic field affects **solar flares** and the solar wind.

Massive flares of gas erupt from the turbulent surface of the sun in an astonishingly detailed ultraviolet photograph taken by the Solar Dynamics Observatory, launched in 2010.

How Old Is the Sun and When Might It Burn Out?

The sun is about 4.6 billion years old. That is also the approximate age of the **solar system.**

Scientists think the sun began to form when part of a huge, spinning cloud of dust and gas became *denser* (more closely packed) than the region that surrounded it. The **gravity** of this dense region caused the cloud to shrink. As the cloud shrank, the gas in its center squeezed into a ball, making the gas hotter. In time, the center of the ball became hot and dense enough to produce energy by **nuclear fusion**. The ball became a **star** that we call the sun.

The sun, viewed from a burned-out Earth, appears as a red dwarf in an artist's illustration (left). The moon is passing between the sun and Earth.

The sun has enough **hydrogen** in its **core** to continue **radiating** energy for another 5 billion years. The sun is in the yellow dwarf phase of a star's life. After the hydrogen is gone, the sun will become larger and brighter for a time. It will become a red giant. The sun's outer layers will drift into space. The remaining core, called a white dwarf, will slowly fade to become a faint, cool object known as a black dwarf (see page 46).

Highlights

- The sun is about 4.6 billion years old.
- Scientists expect the sun to shine as it does now for another 5 billion years.
- Eventually the sun will burn more brightly for a time. Then its outer layers will drift into space and it will cool down.

How Far Away Are the Stars?

The **star** closest to Earth is the sun. The sun is, on average, about 93 million miles (150 million kilometers) from Earth. The closest star to the **solar system** is Proxima Centauri. It is more than 25 trillion miles (40 trillion kilometers) from the sun. This distance is so great that it takes 4.2 years for light to travel from there to the sun. For this reason, scientists say that the sun and Proxima Centauri are 4.2 **light-years** apart.

Such distances are very hard to imagine. You could think about them this way: Suppose you had a car that could travel in space. If your car could travel continually at 55 miles (89 kilometers) per hour, it would take about 30 weeks to travel to Earth's moon. It would take about 50 years to travel to Venus; 200 years to travel to the sun; and 5,795 years to travel to distant Neptune. Proxima Centauri is so far away, it would take more than 500 million years to travel there in your space car.

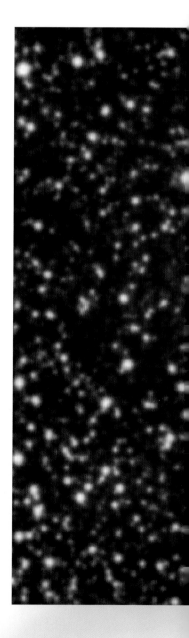

Highlights

- The sun is the star closest to Earth. It is about 93 million miles (150 million kilometers) away.

- The next closest star is Proxima Centauri, which lies 25 trillion miles (40 trillion kilometers) from the sun.

- Scientists often use a measurement called a light-year to describe distances in space. Proxima Centauri is 4.2 light-years from the sun.

A photograph of Proxima Centauri in *infrared* (heat) light

What Do Stars Look Like?

Stars are shaped like a ball and are bright and glowing. Stars other than the sun look like small points of light to us because that they are so far away from Earth.

Stars can be bright or faint in the night sky. How bright a star appears to us depends partly on its distance from Earth. But a star's brightness also depends on its surface temperature and its size. A bigger star gives off more light than a smaller star, even if the two stars have the same surface temperature. A hotter star gives off more light than a cooler star.

Stars come in different colors. If you look carefully at the stars, even without binoculars or a telescope, you will see a range of color from reddish to yellowish to bluish. A star's color depends on its surface temperature. Stars that look blue are the hottest. Stars that look red are the least hot. Those that look yellow—such as the sun—are in-between. Although a star may appear in a single color, it actually gives off a broad **spectrum** (band) of colors.

Not all stars are bright and glowing like our sun. Stars that have burned up all of their fuel, such as white dwarfs, do not shine much at all.

The colors of the stars reveal their temperature in this natural-color photograph.

Highlights

- From Earth, stars look like small points of light because they are so far away.

- Stars that are hotter, larger, or closer to Earth than surrounding stars appear brighter.

- Stars vary in color, depending on their temperature. Stars that look blue are the hottest. Red stars are the least hot.

How Big Are Stars?

Astronomers measure the size of **stars** by comparing them with the sun's **radius.** The sun's radius is about 432,000 miles (695,500 kilometers). The largest stars, called supergiants, can have a radius of 650 million miles (1 billion kilometers) or more. That is approximately 1,500 times as great as the sun's radius. The supergiant Antares is about 700 solar radii (the plural of radius). That means Antares has a radius roughly 700 times

A red dwarf is usually from 1/12 to 1/2 times as small as the sun.

Highlights

- Astronomers measure the size of stars by comparing their radius to that of the sun. A star's size is expressed in solar radii (the plural of radius).

- The largest stars, which can have a radius of 650 million miles (1 billion kilometers) or more, are called supergiants.

- Stars like the sun, which has a radius of 432,000 miles (695,500 kilometers), are called dwarfs.

Comparing Star Size

A supergiant star can be 1,500 or more times as large as the sun.

The sun is a yellow dwarf star.

larger than the sun's radius. But Proxima Centauri, the star closest to Earth except for the sun, measures only 0.145 solar radii. Its radius is only 14 percent as large as the sun's.

Astronomers classify the sun as a dwarf star. Dwarf stars are not all small, but scientists call them "dwarfs" because other types of stars are much larger. Both the sun and Proxima Centauri are dwarfs.

What Are Stars Made Of?

Stars consist mainly of **hydrogen,** which has the lightest *nucleus* (center) of all chemical elements. Nearly all of the rest of a star's **mass** is made up of helium, the second lightest element. Small amounts of a few other elements make up the remaining mass.

As stars age, they *fuse* (combine) helium nuclei to create such heavier elements as carbon, oxygen, neon, and silicon. Supergiant stars are factories for the production of even heavier elements, including gold and lead. At the end of its life, a supergiant explodes with tremendous violence in a supernova. This explosion creates heavy elements and shoots them into space. Most of the elements that make up Earth originated in supernova explosions.

Fun Fact

A "shooting star" that blazes across the sky is not a star at all but a meteoroid that burns up as it enters Earth's atmosphere.

Highlights

- Hydrogen makes up most of the mass of a star.
- Helium makes up most of the rest of the mass.
- Supergiant stars are chemical factories for the production of heavier elements.
- Most of the chemical elements that make up Earth originated in supernova explosions.

A cloud of gas called the Southern Ring Nebula appears in a false-color photograph. The cloud formed when the star at its center (arrow) blew off its outer layers.

Why Do Stars Shine?

Stars shine in a
natural-color photograph

Stars shine for the same reason that the sun does. They give off energy in the forms of heat and light. Most of this energy is produced through a process called **nuclear fusion** deep inside the star's **core.**

In the core, the *nuclei* (centers) of **hydrogen** atoms continually crash into one another. When they collide, the nuclei *fuse* (combine) to form the nucleus of a heavier kind of atom, helium. This nuclear fusion reaction releases huge amounts of energy. In the process, the star gets very hot and gives off light.

Stars shine in Earth's sky all day and night. During the day, the sun's bright light overpowers the faint light from other stars. We can see these other stars only at night when the sky is dark and clear.

Highlights

- Stars shine as they release energy as heat and light.
- A star's energy comes from nuclear fusion reactions in its core.
- During a nuclear fusion reaction, hydrogen atoms crash into each other. Their nuclei fuse, changing the hydrogen to helium and releasing some of the energy as heat and light.

The Sun and Other Stars **35**

How Are Stars Classified?

Astronomers *classify* (group) **stars** by various characteristics. Such characteristics include size and **mass** (amount of **matter**).

Stars are also classified by color. On a *spectral* (color) chart (right, top), stars are grouped into classes based on their surface temperature. The classes are, from hottest to coolest, O, B, A, F, G, K, M, and L.

Stars are further organized by *luminosity* (the rate at which they give off light and other forms of energy). These classifications range from brightest to least bright, with the designations Ia, Ib, II, III, IV, and V (see chart right, bottom).

Such designations allow astronomers to compare stars. For instance, the sun belongs to the class G2V. This means that the sun is a dwarf star (V) in the yellow (G) **spectrum** and is relatively hot (2). The star Alpha Centauri is also a G2V. So, we know that these two stars share some characteristics.

Highlights

- Stars are classified according to such characteristics as size, mass, color, surface temperature, and luminosity.
- Each class is assigned a letter or number that allows astronomers to quickly identify and compare stars with one another.

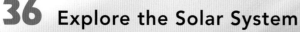

Classifying Stars

The chart at the top of this page shows a classification system based on the color of a star, which is related to a star's surface temperature. The chart at the bottom of this page classifies stars according to their brightness.

Color Classification

Spectral class			
O	Hottest blue stars	Hottest stars
B	Hot blue stars	
A	Blue/blue-white stars	
F	White stars	
G	Yellow stars	
K	Orange-red stars	
M	Red stars	
L	Coolest red stars	Coolest stars

Luminosity Classification

Ia	Bright supergiants	Brightest stars
Ib	Supergiants	
II	Bright giants	
III	Giants	
IV	Subgiants	
V	Main sequence or dwarf	Faintest stars

How Hot Are Stars?

Stars are very, very hot. **Astronomers** measure star temperatures using a metric unit called the **kelvin** (abbreviated K).

The **core** temperatures of stars can range from about 10 million K to nearly 10 billion K. At the high end of this range are collapsing stars that are about to explode as supernovas (see page 48).

A ring of hot blue stars surrounds a ball of older, cooler yellow stars in a natural-color photograph taken by the Hubble Space Telescope (below).

Highlights

- The temperature of a star is expressed in a metric unit called the kelvin (K).

- The core temperatures of stars range from 10 million K to about 10 billion K.

- The surface temperatures of stars range from abut 2,500 K to about 50,000 K.

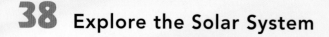

Stars also have different surface temperatures. Red stars have a surface temperature that ranges from about 2,500 K to 3,500 K. The sun and other yellow stars have a surface temperature of about 5,500 K. Surface temperatures for blue stars range from about 10,000 K to 50,000 K.

Bluish-white hot, young stars fill the centers of two galaxies (left and below). They are surrounded by cooler, older reddish-white stars in a natural-color photograph taken by the Hubble Space Telescope.

How Old Are Stars?

The oldest **stars** are thought to be between 12 billion and 13 billion years old. New stars are being born all the time.

Stars, like people, have life cycles. Stars are born, pass through several stages of life, and die. Some stars end their lives by fading slowly. Others explode violently.

The life cycle of a star depends on its **mass** at the beginning of its life, measured in comparison with the sun. High-mass stars form quickly, burn very hot, and have short lives for stars—often less than 10 million years. Intermediate-mass stars like the sun may last for tens of billions of years.

Low-mass stars have a low surface temperature and use fuel so slowly that they may live for hundreds of billions of years. This expected life span is longer than the present age of the universe, calculated to be about 13.7 billion years. For this reason, scientists believe that so far no low-mass star has died by running out of fuel.

Highlights

- A star's life cycle depends on its mass at birth.
- Stars of low mass compared to the sun burn slowly and may live for more than 1 trillion years.
- Intermediate-mass stars burn more quickly and last for billions of years.
- High-mass stars burn hot but have the shortest lives.

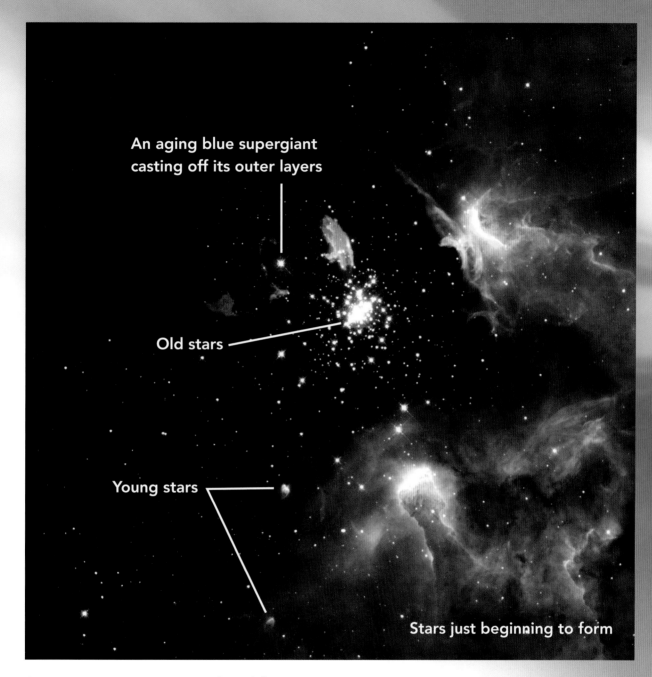

An aging blue supergiant casting off its outer layers

Old stars

Young stars

Stars just beginning to form

Stars at various stages in their life cycle in a natural-color photograph made by combining several images

What Kind of Star Is the Sun?

Astronomers classify the sun as an intermediate-**mass star.** Intermediate-mass stars range from about ½ of a solar mass to 8 solar masses.

The sun is about 4.6 billion years old. It is in its **main-sequence phase.** During this stage, a star still gets energy from **nuclear fusion reactions** involving **hydrogen** in its **core.**

The sun will stay in that phase for about another 5 billion years. Then it will expand to become a red giant (see page 45).

After the sun has run out of fuel, it will cast off its outer layers. It will leave behind a glowing core called a white dwarf. As this white dwarf cools, it will fade. It will become a dark, cold object called a black dwarf (see page 46).

Highlights

- The sun is an intermediate-mass star.
- At this time in its life cycle, the sun still gets energy from nuclear fusion reactions in its core.
- Scientists believe the sun will continue to fuse hydrogen for 5 billion more years before becoming a red giant.
- After it has run out of fuel, the sun will become a white dwarf and then a black dwarf.

A photograph of the sun in ultraviolet light

Fun Fact

Astronomers estimate that there are about 200 billion to 400 billion stars in the Milky Way Galaxy.

The Sun and Other Stars 43

What Is a Red Giant?

A swirling cloud of dust surrounds a red giant at the outer edge of the Milky Way Galaxy in a photograph by the Hubble Space Telescope.

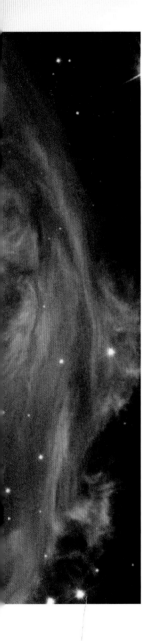

A red giant is a large, intermediate-mass **star** with a bright, reddish glow. When all the **hydrogen** in the **core** of an intermediate-mass star has *fused* (combined) into helium, changes rapidly occur inside the star. The star begins to expand enormously.

As the star swells, its outer layers become cooler, so the star becomes redder and brighter. The star is now a red giant.

The red-giant stage is the beginning of the end for a star. This stage may last a few hundred million to a few billion years.

Highlights

- A red giant is a large, intermediate-mass star nearing the end of its life cycle.
- The red giant stage begins when all of the hydrogen in the star's core has been changed into helium.
- A star may remain in the red giant stage from a few hundred million years to a few billion years.

What Are White Dwarfs and Black Dwarfs?

A white dwarf and a black dwarf represent the final two stages in the life cycle of intermediate-mass **stars** like the sun. These stages occur after the red-giant stage.

A white dwarf is a star that has burned up all of its fuel. Such a star consists mostly of the carbon and oxygen that remain at the **core** after the star has cast off its outer layers. A white dwarf is too faint to be seen without a telescope.

White dwarfs are not actually white. Their color may range from violet to deep red, depending on their surface temperature.

Eventually, a white dwarf stops glowing and becomes a dark, cinder-like object called a black dwarf. The **universe** is so young that few if any stars have existed long enough to become black dwarfs. But **astronomers** believe that stars will become black dwarfs in the future.

Highlights

- A star becomes a white dwarf when it has burned up all its fuel. It becomes a black dwarf when it no longer shines at all.
- White dwarfs are mostly made up of carbon and oxygen.
- A white dwarf is actually violet to deep red in color. It is usually too faint to be seen without a telescope.

A white dwarf in an artist's illlustration

White dwarf

What Is a Supernova?

A supernova is an exploding **star.** It is the last stage in the life of a high-**mass** star. A high-mass star is hot and blue. As it dies, the star's outer layers slowly cool, and the star swells into a red supergiant. After a time, the star collapses suddenly and then violently explodes as a supernova.

The exploded star can become billions of times as bright as the sun before fading from view. A supernova explosion throws a large cloud of gas and dust into space. New stars may form from the gas and dust.

Astronomers classify supernovae (the plural of supernova) into two types. A Type II supernova results from the death of a single massive star. Astronomers believe the Type I kind probably occurs in binary stars, a pair of closely paired stars that **orbit** each other.

A supernova in a false-color photograph made by combining images from several telescopes

Highlights

- A supernova is the last stage in a high-mass star's life.
- As a star becomes a supernova, it becomes hotter and swells. Then it collapses and explodes.
- High-mass stars change color from blue to red as they become supernovas.
- New stars may form from the cloud of gas and dust left over after a supernova explosion.

What Is a Neutron Star?

Bright X rays surround a pulsar in a close-up of the central area of a neutron star.

When a high-**mass star** explodes as a supernova, it sometimes leaves behind a small, dense spinning **core.** That object is called a neutron star. (A dense object has particles packed tightly together.)

Neutron stars have a mass of up to three times that of the sun. This mass is packed into a ball with a **radius** of only about 6 to 10 miles (10 to 15 kilometers).

A neutron star is so small that its visible light is difficult to see. But these stars also send out radio waves. Neutron stars that send out radio waves in regular pulses are called **pulsars.**

Scientists predicted the existence of neutron stars in 1938. It was not until 1967, however, that neutron stars were actually discovered by **astronomers** using special telescopes. These telescopes were able to detect radio waves.

Highlights

- A neutron star is the small, dense object left behind when a high-mass star explodes as a supernova.
- Neutron stars are very difficult to see. They are usually detected by the radio waves that they send out.
- A neutron star that sends out radio waves in regular pulses is called a pulsar.

What Is a Black Hole?

A black hole is an area of space where **gravity** is so strong that nothing can escape from it. Black holes are invisible because not even light can escape.

Black holes form from the leftover **core** of an exploding **star** called a supernova. If the core has more than three times as much **mass** as that of the sun, the core collapses inward in a fraction of a second. All the star's mass disappears into a single tiny point. This point is smaller than the *nucleus* (center) of an **atom.**

We cannot see a black hole directly. But we can see its effect on the **orbits** of stars and other objects that are drawn toward it. Scientists believe that an extremely massive black hole lies at the center of most **galaxies.**

Black holes may also produce **radiation** that can be seen by certain types of telescopes. Scientists think that gas falling into a black hole is heated to extreme temperatures. The gas gives off jets of X rays that **astronomers** can detect.

Highlights

- A black hole is a place in space where gravity is so strong that even light cannot escape from it.
- Black holes form if the core left over from a supernova explosion is so massive that it collapses.
- Scientists find black holes by seeing their effects on nearby objects or by spotting jets of radiation in space.

Hot gas that gives off X rays surrounds the supermassive black hole (arrow) known as Sagittarius A* at the center of the Milky Way Galaxy.

What Are Binary Stars?

Binary **stars** are pairs of stars that are close together and **orbit** around each other. They hold each other captive by the force of **gravity.** Most binaries are so close that, from Earth, they look like single stars. Some stars in a binary system appear to orbit an invisible companion that may be a black hole.

Sometimes a binary star pulls **matter** from its companion star. In that case, the expanding star can grow large enough to shine extremely brightly or even explode.

From 50 to 75 percent of all stars are binary stars. However, the sun is not a binary star. The closest binary star system to Earth is made up of Alpha Centauri A and Alpha Centauri B. These stars are about 4.4 **light-years** from Earth.

Matter flows from a large, sun-like star (opposite page) to a white dwarf (above) in an artist's illustration of a binary system.

What Is a Brown Dwarf?

A brown dwarf is a dim object in space that failed to become a **star**. Brown dwarfs have more **mass** than a **planet** but less mass than a star. All known brown dwarfs are all about the same size as the planet Jupiter. But they have a much greater **mass**.

Highlights

- Brown dwarfs are dim objects that are about the size of Jupiter but have much more mass than Jupiter does.
- Brown dwarfs form the same way that stars do. But because they do not have enough mass, they never become hot enough to be a star.
- Brown dwarfs eventually shrink, cool, and fade.

A brown dwarf forms the same way a star does—from a huge, swirling cloud of gases and dust in space. The cloud shrinks into a ball, spins, and heats up. The warmest and brightest brown dwarfs glow a dull red and resemble low-mass stars called red dwarfs. But a brown dwarf does not have enough mass to get hot enough to become a star. Instead, it continues to shrink, and then cools and fades.

A brown dwarf and its moon orbit a triple-star system in an artist's illustration.

How Do Stars and Groups of Stars Get Their Names?

Stars that have a name usually have been important to people in some way. Perhaps the star is very bright in the night sky, like the star Sirius. Or, the star may be used by travelers to find their way. For example, Polaris, also called the North Star, has long been used by navigators.

For thousands of years, people have seen patterns in the stars. For some people, the stars have appeared in the shape of animals. Other patterns have reminded stargazers of people or objects. These patterns of stars, called **constellations,** have often been named for animals or people in myths and legends. The constellation Ursa Major, meaning *Great Bear,* was named for an ancient Greek myth. Most constellations were named long ago.

Stars discovered today are identified by letters and numbers by the International Astronomical Union (IAU). The letters at the beginning of each label indicate the type of star. For example, the label PSR J1302-6350 indicates that this star is a rotating object in space called a **pulsar.** The letters and numbers that follow tell **astronomers** the star's location in the sky.

Highlights

- Many stars and constellations were named long ago, because they were important to people in some way.
- Today, newly discovered stars are named by the International Astronomical Union (IAU).
- The IAU assigns a code name to stars, based on the type of star they are and their position in the sky.

Some well-known constellations

Cygnus

Cepheus

Andromeda

Cassiopeia

Ursa Minor

Draco

Ursa Major

Glossary

asteroid A small body made of rock, carbon, or metal that orbits the sun. Most asteroids are between the orbits of Mars and Jupiter.

astronomer A scientist who studies stars and planets.

atmosphere The gases that surround a planet or star.

atom One of the basic units of matter.

comet A small body made of dirt and ice that orbits the sun.

constellation A pattern of stars visible in a particular region of the night sky.

core The center part of the inside of a planet or star.

coronal mass ejection An eruption of large amounts of material from the sun's corona into space.

diameter The distance of a straight line through the middle of a circle or anything shaped like a ball.

electron A negatively charged particle that forms part of an atom.

galaxy A system of billions of stars.

gravity The effect of a force of attraction that acts between all objects because of their mass.

hydrogen The most abundant chemical element in the universe.

ion An atom or a group of atoms that has an electric charge.

kelvin A metric unit used to measure temperatures. The Kelvin scale starts at absolute zero—the temperature at which scientists think that atoms have the least possible energy.

light-year The distance that light travels in one year, equal to about 5.88 trillion miles (9.46 trillion kilometers).

magnetic field The space around a magnet or magnetized object within which its power of attraction works.

main-sequence phase The stage in the life cycle of a star at which the star gets all its energy from hydrogen fusion reactions in its core.

mass The amount of matter a thing contains.

matter The substance, or material, of which all objects are made.

nuclear fusion reaction A process by which two atomic nuclei join to create a new, larger nucleus; these reactions produce energy in such stars as the sun.

orbit The path that a smaller body takes around a larger body, such as the path that a planet takes around the sun. Also, to travel in an orbit.

planet A large, round body in space that orbits a star. A planet must have sufficient gravitational pull to clear other objects from the area of its orbit.

plasma A form of matter similar to gas, made up of positively charged ions and of negatively charged electrons.

proton A positively charged particle that forms part of an atom.

pulsar An object in space that gives off regular bursts—or pulses—of electromagnetic radiation. Most of this radiation is in the form of radio waves.

radiation Energy given off in the form of waves or small particles of matter.

radius Any line going straight from the center to the outside of a circle or sphere. The distance from the center of a star to its surface is a star's radius.

satellite An artificial satellite is an object built by people and launched into space. Most satellites continually orbit Earth or some other body.

solar flare A sudden brightening of a part of the solar atmosphere during which a tremendous amount of energy is released.

solar system A group of bodies in space made up of a star and the planets and other objects orbiting that star.

spectrum A band of visible light, or some other kind of radiation, arranged in order of wavelength. (Wavelength is the distance between successive wave crests, or tops of waves.) A rainbow is a spectrum. Its bands range from red, which contains particles of light with the least amount of energy, to violet, which contains the most energetic particles.

star A huge, shining ball in space that produces a tremendous amount of visible light and other forms of energy.

sunspot A dark, circular feature on the solar surface.

universe Everything that exists anywhere in space and time.

For More Information

Books

Sun:

Far-out Science Projects About Earth's Sun and Moon by Robert Gardner (Enslow Elementary, 2008)

The Sun by Elaine Landau (Children's Press, 2008)

The Sun by Steve Parker (Rosen Central, 2008)

Stars:

Constellations by Flora Kim (Children's Press, 2010)

Extreme Stars! (Smithsonian Institution and Collins, 2006)

The Stars by David Jefferis (Crabtree Publishing, 2009)

Web sites

Sun:

NASA's Solar System Exploration: Sun
http://sse.jpl.nasa.gov

National Geographic's Science and Space: Sun
http://science.nationalgeographic.com

Stars:

National Geographic's Science and Space: Stars
http://science.nationalgeographic.com

Stars: Protostars, Bright Stars, Red Giants, White Dwarfs
http://www.geocities.com